Letting in the Blue

J. Ryan.

Janet Ryan

Letting in the Blue
Janet Ryan

Published in November 2021
Buff Press
20 Clovelly Way, Orpington,
Kent, BR6 0WD
ISBN 978-1-7398102-0-7

Cover Design: *Reaching High*, © Anne Stewart, 2021
Author Photo: *Janet Ryan at Shortlands Poetry Circle Centenary, 2011*, © Isabel Turvey

to Tom Ryan (i.m. 2012)

Forever grateful for taking me
to all the worlds we visited together.

Acknowledgements

thanks are due to the editors of the following
where several of these poems first appeared:

each passing breeze, Envoi,
Perspectives, Soundings, the rainbow comes and goes

and to the following, whose encouragement
has been invaluable:

Isabel Bermudez, Roger Elkin, Jean Ellis,
and Anne Stewart

and to the readers and writers of the Shortlands Poetry Circle
for their friendship and support.

Contents

Open to the page when…

in a house on wheels
the three squash together
at a table, elbow each other
into shy giggles at passing glances
and smiles through the window.

Pulling partitions
between their worlds
they savour the newness
of souvenirs in their own space
pocket them in the dark reaches
of a drawer.

Feeling the rasp of a cow's tongue
salt-sweat on hands, the diminutive three
see themselves in the blue-black
depths of her eye.

In early hours while eels simmer
and aromas tantalise, they
finger-draw faces in condensation
laughter trickling into night.

In a crowded frame
branches net stars
and the three
float in paper light dreams
to fields of a universe stretching away.

Watching Moments

1.

Children tell the hours on learning clocks.
Telling minutes of life stretch before them,
they don't yet feel the pinch of time.

2.

Metal puzzles twist patience,
the child frees pieces
or herself, sighing,

3.

After pre-school
she offers Teddy tea, saying,
We have to look for another Papa
because
and leaning to his ear
shares the whispered secret.

Many A Slip

Don’t go near the edge,
she had told him.
Don’t go near the edge.

How easily it had happened.
For only seconds his gaze had drifted.
He returned with a wet child.

Spluttering. Frilly pants afloat.
She straightened, muddied,
dripping but unfazed.

Brushing detritus from her dress,
copying him, she smiled
with her mother’s lips,

and he heard,
a silent, I told you so.

Some do, some don't

For them
the children
shouting in excitement

as loud as reds, bronze,
scarlets of polyanthus
and wallflowers
near-by.

Now, in the slide queue,
a blond-blue eyed toddler
swivels his head
from one older child
to another, and overbalances.

An older girl,
a seven-year-old 'mother'
picks him up;
all comfort and cuddles,
sets him back on his feet.

Again, the little chap
with an expansive grin
and red cheeks –
not wanting to miss
any words
flying above his head,
looks up.

Lost key

Dressed in our Sunday best,
we ate high-tea
sitting at the barley-twist table.

Mother's stare held us in check.
Locked in controlled silence
we searched every where
but each other's faces
for a focal point
in case we burst
into fits of giggles.

This house, where one word uttered
was too many,
never buzzed with conversation.

No objects of persona' attachment
decorated wall or surface;
all trace of intimate detail
locked away.

Touching

I slid his small fingers
across the top of a pom-pom dahlia.
Laughing at the many cinnamon petals
tickling his skin, he may have
pictured this shape
side by side with a ball.

Then, on to the Japanese anemone,
like a tall, elegant lady
gazing toward a mountain
in the space of air between,
her thoughts a mystery.

And his too just for a second
as he looked up at it;
the dreamy stare into otherness
before sniffing the flower.
I bent to him, he wrinkling
his podgy nose, smiling
in watching moments.

Yes,

so ordinary,
the way we live –
until I hear a cry,
routine takes second place,
calm sets in under pressure.

Another more desperate cry,
a baby girl caught under a fence –
I reach for her and she for me –
and, relaxing,
she comes through
without a whimper.

The old fence board giving up
its captive, her pink blanket
trailing.

Once again

rushing
to the cow-shed
of early morning
just to see the milking,
breathe   warm milk air.

Shapes walking
out of a child's painting;
black continents on cream seas
they amble into the sun,
cleft hooves smoothing
mud into runnels.

Nose to tail in the lane,
finding by habit
the way to grazing.

On our return the next year
the cows were hooked to machines

Where is she now

Glancing through the shop-window
of the red-bricked house
he is drawn by the reflected calm
against a blank of summer blue.

Mesmerised by the message
in a large flowing hand
on a postcard standing
on a Victorian table there
he sees himself with long curls,
in a pinafore dress,
with a pink-pantalooned, bonneted girl.

Bent like pegs stuck in sand
they fumble for elusive crabs
together. Never a day passing
but that she asks him to explore

Novelty Wears

Passers-by see them as first-year infants;
wide-eyed, smiling, diminutive as dolls
in uniforms sized for next year
cuffs caught round knuckles
hem-lines down to mid-shin.

Others
with watery eyes cling
and hang back –
today is too new.

Tomorrow
they will wander home
behind their parents
shirt-tails hanging out
shoes scuffed
loose laces flicking.

All change

Young girls hunch
under an unruly umbrella,
struggle against
blustery showers.

Autumn nips.
Sleeves cover sunburn,
Summer is packed away
with shorts and flimsy shift.

Conkers shine like polished wood
until boys bag them.

Plants wither, leaves blacken
in the grasp of frost;
silhouetted veins stand out
against a pale sun.
The earth, trees wait.

Plum Jam

Tempted by the plump fruit,
ripened skins of star-blown magenta,
nebulous in the purple darks of space,
school boys fill blazer pockets
while wasps buzz round their heads.

Chasing through avenues
of spotted shade, they pelt each other,
squashed pulp dripping,
conscience stains on white.

Tired of mischief,
wandering homeward
they pull at damp shirts
sticking to their backs,
claw blindly at itches
they cannot reach. At home
Mother serves them guilt for tea.

Every small detail

After looking at just one
patch of blue, just a promise,
she thinks, noticing the return
of two swans, their serenity
in companionship.

Later cold fingers yellowing;
grasping a hot coffee cup
she's safely masked,
not too close to faces
of others nearby
at the café.

Missing the spice of lives
hearing known and unknown
voices there, echoes
of shaped lines
come to her on the wind.

And now
seeing a Syrian woman
begging; head wrapped
against the freezing night
passed sitting on the pavement,
she sips her coffee slowly
thinking of her
worry about
children left behind.

Bread and Wine

Creeping over us
as if drinking wine,
 a relaxed mood;
 a constant trickle

the bubble of people's laughter,
so often heard
in the comfort
of the cafe,
in the warmth
of mingling voices
rising and falling
like a young stream
over stones.
From the opposite table

strangers tell of their lives,
the bread of different days.
For what is it that compels
us to search out

another's tales
of happiness? They want you
to listen to their anecdotes.
They are facing what we fear.

Closer to home

She has never stopped
looking at the stars

shining through nebulae
cerise overlaid on purple
clouds of dust
and gas, stuff of the future
streaming around the galaxy.

Wired voices
across unknown paths
think nebulae
an artist's dream.

Now,
touching the stone arch
of a bombed monastery
she catches daylight
and the brittle
war-filled centuries

but of a sudden
she cannot
relate to the age
of the stars.

They are too far to fathom.

Expectation doused

Copper – gold birch leaves net
the blue as I pass
treading flat clusters
blown down in last night's gale.

Grass glistens as I step aside
to allow distancing from walkers'
excited rat-sized dogs.

I am reminded
that at this o'clock
no chance of cutting grass
would arise today,

only maybe a patch of weeding
to urge myself on tomorrow.

Looking up
to see
specks of rain fall
in quick succession,
the sky now yellowing-grey;

umbrellas zoom up,
sheen wet in an instant
and the rat-sized dogs
don't look
so chipper anymore.

Watching

the cushioning, feathering
of silver-tipped clouds
lowering the setting sun

into dusk, and distracted
by a male swan,
wings flapping loud,
harrying his two young

from the lake, his territory,
she later tells two friends this.
And is visited by
the whispered question

that insists in her mind;
was that yesterday?

Turning back the summers

He conjured long light evenings
to play his trumpet at the bandstand.
At least, we thought so,
but as we learned later
he was changing the hour,
and only Grandad
touched the clock.

He farmed carp, watching them rise,
selectively tasting crumbs,
milling in his shadow,
long strong ovals of gold,
bridging the surface.

The clock, taken for granted,
a background noise
still chimes, pendulum,
keen as a metronome,
marking quick-march time.

We've been there too

Here
In the shade of shimmering leaves
floral print dresses
freshen the haze
like a breeze.

And there
contrasting with her tan
in a little black number
she displays
an air of panache,

her man
clumsy in flip-flops
sports shorts
an open-necked shirt
undone to the waist
carries a six-pack of beer.

The olds watch, reflect.
'Beach or party in the park?'

Nearly There

Through binoculars the poplars
like birch brooms sweeping the sky
are splashed with dots of green shoots
brightening winter's drab.

And overcast March threatens snow
though not holding back Spring's collection;
in the photographer's dream still
the daffodil, tulip and leafy bluebell
blooming in the sometime burst of sun rays.

We wait, watch for late-sown shoots
hoping the hidden future will surprise
in spite of menacing frost.

Wound Up

Expecting a short spell of silence,
we sit on the train, stretched scarves
of pink willowherb and yarrow waving us off.

In a crisp voice resounding through the carriage,
diverting thought from the printed page,
or office agenda, the young lady chats
to her mobile as if she had caught
the world by the tail.

'I highlight a full head of hair.
Oh, it is easy.
I ask the client for her colour of choice,
the same or a complete change,
I offer everything, then I can charge...'

Her words keep coming, interrupting tensions
like a key winding up a clock, then stops,
she prevents them resuming their line
of thought. Seats away

a cough punctuates her sentences, papers titter
under her nose. She rises and still talking,
steps out. As the doors close
relief creeps back in with a sigh.

Café comment

And he walks out
of the café as if
he has a vested interest
there.

Traffic rushing by
is of no concern
as he takes a sip
of his latte

and returns later
finding his order so good
compliments the cook
on the Chicken Wrap

on how he'd made it
so hot, hot, hot.

Tea at Browns

Richly ingrained,
the intrigues of a century
steeped in scrolled oak-panel walls.

Chandeliers gently illuminate
to the last tear-drop,
enhancing folds
of green and gold curtain.
She leans, feeling the comfort
of a deeply curved armchair.

The cream bone-china tea set
shines like a display not to be touched
yet nursing an exquisite cup,
the gold rim underlined
with a green circle,
closed by a single rose,
she sips slowly, senses
a past of enjoyed wealth
in this moment

while Mozart fills
the atmosphere,
trickles into pockets
of silence

and she is back
in a Victorian afternoon.

Flapper Days

young girls saunter in
out of the rain, wearing
short camisoles
tight jeans
exposing bejewelled belly-buttons,
careless of the weather's mood.

Shaking her head
a granny tuts, forgetting
the Black-Bottom dance;
knees exposed, long beads
and tassels at her breast twirling.

In a sequined skull cap,
a shimmer of colour,
she danced 'til dawn
and like the stars
sparkled silver
through the trees.

Beating the odds

… have to beat the rain
coming with the wind –
a beautiful day –
shame not to sweep.

Out with the broom;
          push   puush –
muscles tightening
all the way down;
more useful than I thought.

Glancing back,
satisfaction creeps in
for a job and now,
when tomorrow pours
I will grin.

Moments when the clock stops

Days unfold with slow drips on the sill,
and I long to be in warmer air.

Winter's dull face
turns me from the mist
hanging around houses,
hedges; edges a blur,
a washed out old 'photo.

Starved of definition
I look at a painting.

Uplifted by wisps of smoke
from a stone house on hilly moorland,
the horizon a rush of white cloud
stacking on blue,
sunspots catch bell heather dancing,
cotton grasses waving; and there
a blond-haired child throwing
seeds to bantams
running to her.

Brilliant coxcomb
to iridescence of tail feathers
satisfying my senses
but now, leaning forward
to grasp the poetry
in the smooth passage

of her daily chore, I feel
the morning stops
for the smile of this girl
hoping for a brown egg
for breakfast.

Encounters

Head under wing, eleven herons doze
in the ghostly half-lit shadow
of poplars, oblivious to passing traffic
alongside in the country lane.

Coach tourists climb down
crowd the restaurant,
bursting bubbles of reflection
in quiet corners.

Further on, woodland paths pond
in holes gouged by off-roader wheels,
an impassable wasteland. No longer
scattered scarves of winding colours;
poppies, cornflowers, pimpernels.

Stubborn sheep jump slate walls
stopping us in our tracks,
strangely aloof, staring
at our being there.

The pocket of Middleham

Towering over
old grey stone cottages
the ruins of the castle
of Richard III
still stands strong.

Round the cobbled square
echoes of a racing string,
eager for the spring of turf
bounces off walls,
and dawns on waking ears.

Reflecting on slate tiles
the glint on a wave of roofs
is broken by dormers
yawning wide to the sun.

A scrabble pattern of paving
serves the guest house kitchen,
breakfast frying.

Spare time gigs

Passers-by see
as youngsters sing
to 'Jailhouse Rock',
themselves living it up
in their day in discos

in another world;
strobe lights lift clothes
to iridescence
and with such youthful energy
some couldn't quite see
in themselves now.

Further on
a harlequin-suited mime
with time hanging
on his every imperceptible move,
children cajoling him
to blink though they fall silent
held in the mirror of his eye.

The juggler, five balls in the air
nonchalantly chats
to a breath-held crowd
as if his act were no part of him;

and the olds looking on
picture the poor back in time;
the silent ask for money
dropped
in the upside down flat-cap.

Out there

our expectancy of magic, but not
a whispering of demons.

While night suspends us
in sleep, an owl hoots,
the soft mystery of silence
across the hill-field.

A hotchpotch of
gasses, dust,
the sneezes of old planets
churn into bubbles,
steam and ripple
in black reaches
among stars,
like the whirlpool
in a cauldron waiting
for the wand to wave,
the spell, to weave,
the recipe of life.

Rambling

So I ignore the knock
of stone pebbles
a drop down the bank
where quite unmoved, terrapins watch
with pre-historic stare
as I pick my steps over roots.

Woodland blurs
I stoop among clumps of violets
stay still.

A green woodpecker
fills my vision
its soft stabbing into earth
drumming in my ear
compelling me to strain forward
probe into that dark hole
just off the normal path.

Each other

He takes his permit back,
shakes in fear of what might meet him.

Robed, mindful of the noon heat,
he hurries, ready to promise anything
to hug his family
again; desperate
as if it will be
for the last time.

In silence,
uncertain of the next step
away from the edge
of far-flung shattered sticks
of chairs
ripped blackened clothes;
debris of their home
but his family wait

then
run to him,
tears fall,
smiles breaking.

Witness

to our late evening walk,
the moon, touched by man,
yet still holds sway
in the dreamer's eye,
reflects in a dusty puddle on the levee.

We hold hands even tighter
as, 'hip hop' music blasting from their cars,
black youths shout
to a scantily clad girl
tottering on high cork-heeled sandals
like a foal on new legs.

Ignored, their obscenities
echo back to them.

Kimswick, Mississippi

Wind whistles through shiplap,
raises the shingles, releasing them
one after the other like piano keys,
people pull up their collars against its chill.

The owners of boarded up log cabins
moved away or gone over,
memories of them thinning to shadow.

Its dusty floor once walked by hob-nail boot
the miner's museum draws tourists
to sense the ache, the running sweat
of pitching a pick into lead seam,
the wearing strain, day after day, shortening life.

Struggling to remain on the tourist route
Kimswick adopted the afternoon tea-shop,
darkly-beamed rooms lending quaintness
to leisure hours.

Restaurants replaced 'old world' farm tools
with sparse displays of pottery,
adding attraction for those searching
to fill a corner in their kitchen

And so this settlement, while humming
with a curiosity about its antiquity,
steps into the present.

Found Wandering

Peppered with gold dust
bees buzz round a bowl of azaleas.
Dark red maple leaves blur
in a breeze, patterning
the far blue.

In an Alice whirl of thought
I hear the cry of yesterday's child
snatched by a tornado,
dropped in mud.

Wiping sludge from her eyes
a policeman's face streams
with tears as she reaches out.

Different outlooks, same days.

Walking briskly
we turn into a cul-de-sac
beech leaves scuttle
downhill en masse
like an army of beetles
with a nor' easterly breeze
following.

Batmobile waits on the lawn
red lights flashing.
Miniature Batman jumps in;
'vrmmm, vrmmm,'
he's ready
for the get-go
into another episode.

Net curtains askew
inside a dark cedar
ship-lapped house
the shadows beyond intrigue;
a 'no trespassing' sign
freezes our stares.

While further on
without thought of tomorrow's fall
a gardener sweeps, bins leaves
his effort fostering pride
in a backward glance.

Sink of Iniquity

A cracking
on the ceiling wakes us.
Ugliness punctuates minutes
waiting for it to stop.

Any second
the cockroach will fall
soundless to the bed
but it didn't land there,
the feel of filth creeps over us.

Gorging itself on cake crumbs
shaken into the sink,
a delicacy before death
as the 'roach
is deftly sped
to the Hereafter.

Seasons

They feel the uplift
and into the clouds are adrift
in weightless dreams.

Later, at plane windows
seeing mirrored the flames
of a Missouri sunset
in reservoirs, flooded field –

but what they didn’t see
unaware of torrential rain
changing rivers into monsters
unearthing trees
sweeping houses
from footings
with no regard
for human struggle;
a power carrying all
before, reaching out
fingers of destruction.

A body of leaves,
tonguing;
a snake slithering
around gutters
might turn their heads
at home

but this
left them
in a silent jaw-
dropping disbelief.

Crowning Touch

Stir-frying
onions, garlic, sliced beef
with red, orange and yellow peppers
bright as the bells of twirling Mexican skirts.

Spicing with coriander,
cumin, chilli and paprika,
aromas rise
spices setting my throat on fire.

Chilled beer cools from inside out.

Satisfied, I sigh. From a high perch
a Red Cardinal, crest fully fanned,
watches a female flying towards him.
His song filling the evening air.

Snow birds

It’s morning.
She watches the cowboy
pass the snow line;
wearing a poncho,
kerchief covering his ears
tying his hat down,
he is over the worst
and would savour
warmth ahead.

She’s here, in her house.
It’s hot as an oven,
wind whistling;
sand-devils breaking in, pushing
through unstopped cracks.

She flinches
remembering her mother
is coming;
no chance now
for a trip to the island
where sea breezes play.

Coming Back

Polishing the maple stair, she keeps busy
tries not to remind herself of her husband
donning grey, leaving to fight
the cause of the cotton-picking slaves.

On the cream satin heading of a yellow blanket
she embroiders stem stitch, linking leaf to bud
recalls sentences from him
writing of his return soon from the blast of cannon.

Her keepsake doll, a foot-soldier
with sword raised, but dressed in blue
like her son, sits on the curved lid
of her work box. Clutching the doll
she watches at the window.

It would take a miracle

Floods like magma
lit red by the town's neon
stealing under sand-bagged doors
seeps higher
higher by the hour.

Prayers unanswered
suffering victims evacuate
thinking even as dinghies
taxi them to safety
the promised help
of a previous year
came too late.

Misplaced pride
their inner sense
of belonging shattered
blows away with night

though inch long buds
point with unfailing fingers
towards a brightly blooming
magnolia Spring.

This caps all

Hidden in snow
downwind where no seal
could scent him
the Inuit waits
near the ice hole

waits…

for the slightest wriggle
of the rod. Across the ice plain
the hunter's day;
his family's needs
at the end of the line.

A nudge… breath held
adrenalin pulsing
not even thinking.

Yes – the line jumps;
dinner it is.

This beats city living.

Extremes

When wind burns men's faces
and snow fields harden to ice,
the reindeer can no longer scrape for lichens
so they push on to find food.

In worlds apart both migrate
Neither knowing whether they lead
or follow in the White Out
until the mist lifts.

No man idles when camp is struck;
tepees are pulled up on poles, fish
netted in ice holes on the menu for supper.
Empty stomachs soon filled, smiles return.

Rested and ready to move on,
tepees dismantled, stacked on sleighs
harnessed to reindeer, the Nenets look
towards another horizon.

At the counting station, a hundred reindeer
are sold and slaughtered. The herders
cooped in their town houses, long to trek again;
follow the herd, no boundaries in their days.

(NENETS - herdsmen of the Tundra)

At the bus stop

At noon, scent heavy in the heat,
she sells whiting at the crossroads,
guards a basketful between knees
from mewing cats
sneaking from under dry leaves
hanging like tongues.

Shrinking back from her curses,
waving stick, they wait
for that unwatched moment.

Crowding, even on the steps of the bus,
travellers pat money-belts
hidden under t-shirts,
silently assured, they show
no change of expression.

Mountain Station – Kurseong

Sitting on the platform edge, the goat-herder yawns,
marks seconds with his swinging leg
while his goats sleep between the tracks,
long shadows cast patterns of cart wheels

turning on the unmade road. Horns blare,
a gathering side-steps briefly diverted from talk
of Christmas fare. Hands together, touching forehead,
a shop-owner bids 'Namasti' to customers

stepping into sunlight
where a dishevelled woman sits
on the pavement. She coughs, fans away
fume clouds. Litter blows downhill,
heaps insults against her fragile frame.
The shining tin at her feet empty.

Years Later

Pitying the beggars sitting at the gate
you gave them pies once
and now you turn away. Over the years
you heard that some of them
were purposely deformed.

You remember the sacred cows
led to grass. Now they paw
plastics of rotting food,
the rancid odour clinging.

Walking shoeless,
hems held calf-high, people accept
the heavy flood water gushing from
blocked storm drains.

In the squeeze of markets
no space now to admire
but for her discerning eye
the turn of a jewelled ankle,
uncovered as a pleated sari sways.

Dust-coated labourers in loincloths
still chisel millstones by the roadside,
offer food and prayers, give
thanks for the gift of the day,
tarpaulins angled between privacy and the stars.

Watching the window

(Kurseong, India, 1998)

A surprise indeed
to those wearing trainers,
suddenly seeing a sari-ed lady,
sitting on a step,
in a hill town
sticking uppers to soles
of 'N' sports shoes
and stacking behind her
piles of the same
ready to go and
next door, front-house,
a butcher quarters a carcass
while a household member
cooks for any takers
of her mutton curry,
aromas borne on the air;
her magic of spices
wooing customers
to her window.

Cyclone Nargis

No song,
birds have lost their bearings.

Hands bleeding,
people claw in rubble
for their lost ones,
air tormented with their wailing
after the fury of the wind has flattened
miles of their meagre subsistence.

Inflaming their desperation,
soldiers trying to instil order
Refusing aid, the regime of a closed world
cannot be seen to fail; not to reach
the many spread over the flood plains

Clinging to all that's left of their homes,
the few bamboo poles still tied together,
victims in vacant stare, sit, wait.

Monterrey

Cables loop, snaking between
broken pavements, weeds twist
turn from the darkness. Unpaid,
the workforce found jobs elsewhere.

Spanish arches embellish apartments
standing next to the old,
terraced and grey.
Cramped between styles,
a fifteenth-century church
breathes in the borrowed space
of a glass wall opposite.
A pedlar's cart drives slowly

stacked with baskets, daubed pots,
dashed off in a few brush strokes,
the squash, cactus flowers and peppers
in boxes, familiars in whittled textures,
the fattened wooden dog, monkey, rabbit,
and masks of gods come alive
in the day-dreams and songs of desert people.

Lakshmi

Plumping pillows at the hotel,
an air of excitement floats to her
from voices in the foyer.

She watches the new arrivals
sorting postcards
swirled round a statue,
not noticing
that under their fluttering hands

stands a figure
worked in bronze.
How she wants
to disrobe it
of the clutter.

Later,
giving the goddess space
to reveal her own merits
she sees
emanating from the statue's new light,
depths of shape
enriched by darks.

Lakshmi is stepping from the dark
her arm raised
inviting attention.

The unexpected

Set down at an oasis market
she hears gold jingle
from brows of veiled women
stepping sandaled to the sand
in a flow of folds and colour
a bubble of high-pitched chatter.

At a stall she holds an onyx elephant
touching, feeling, its marbled greens
echo the forest fringe
screams of splintering trees
where these giants drag logs;
mahouts up, watching
with gentle acceptance.

In the evening
sun and shadow slowly transform
a sprawl of tents into a yellow ochre
and deep scarlet chequer of dunes.
While she listens to travellers' tales
hands shaping words where language fails.

Salt in the wound

In their blood-lust
for a beheading a mixed crowd
shake fists, shouting,
'Traitor.'

Catherine,
not wanting to go unheard,
declares she will die a Queen
but would rather die
the wife of a Culpepper;
and maybe
consumed by love
for Sir Thomas, she is not mindful
of death as she waits,
neck bared.

Loyalty to him
will perhaps rankle King Henry,
and in red-faced anger, ranting,
he will wish Catherine's head
cut off again and again.

Over time

Ghosts peer through windows
from an otherness behind walls
of Tudor houses. We imagine
their embroidered finery
glinting with gold
as they watch us.

They've had their day;
strutting, keeping the poor
in a misery
worn like shackles.

Now peacocks strut
differently
to the same tune;

courtiers puzzle over
Eastern women in burkas
seeing one world
through veiled slits;
beautiful eyes calm

but their minds
are on fire; woken up
and rankling
against their ancient chains.

Early morning mime

Squeezing through branches
Autumn's orange light
drenches the lake;
warmth chasing mist
up the green slope,
the curtain rises
on a ballet of gulls
their doubles
careening the surface.

Flapping small wings
the clownish coot
spurts after a female
like a clockwork toy;
stretched neck, white
daubed on black head,
a love-arrow darting
in a tulle of spray.

The cormorant plays
the wise man
bottle-body still –
its waiting game.
Watching ripples,
he hungers for a beak full.

Spied through glasses
from a hide,
the funky great-crested grebe
raises his crest
and with eyes kohled
rouged cheeks
passes his mate for life
a gift of green.

Show me the beach

Taking the children
to the beach? I text…

Put your feet
in the shimmering wavelets
spilling over the sand
and send me a picture –
I will wriggle my toes
feel that delicious ice-cold
foam creep on –
sending a tickle
round my ankles.

Boscastle

Lashed by a flash flood
the face of three hundred years
gone in an afternoon.

Jack's boat rises from the table
floats out of the window
through the town
down to the sea.

Ripped up trees.
Cars dip and submerge
like toys tossing
in a deluge.

Company

She used to lean against him
listening
but now in his silence
days pass un-named.

She misses
his talk of yesteryear
when crawling under a table
saved his life, as bombs fell.

Before him
the sunlit wheat
brushed gold
against a stormy backdrop
used to light up his eyes

but now watching sky-larks
spiral upward
into the ether
he hears only
their spirit of song.

Mind Over Matter

She stands unsteady
in a chill sea wind
from across the fields
braces her elbow
stiff with age
to peg clothes, determined
she must not give in.

She notices
the miniature Fuschias
nearly overlooked.

She'd forgotten
for a moment
their sheltered corner
where pink petals suspended
in dark shade
are a fragile surprise.

Beyond this time

Least expected
grief takes over
thought
weighing heavily.

Conscience dives
into depths
where
she'd rather not be.

Her spirits holding
she turns
this paralysis
around
to loneliness.

Not pining for love
beyond reason.

Letting in the blue

Storm-racked branches torn
down, rotting, left gaps
in the canopy;

changes like
the son and his children
blowing kisses
across distancing.

Nana's heart sinking,
partings harder each time,
tearful – as she remembers
the smiles

of how it used to be;
life was fine and
now suddenly isn't,
only maybe

it will come again.
She reaches for her face-mask.

Shaping

Stay home.
roads quieter
less pollution
before the norm returns

Mindful of ourselves
in isolated moments
catching the elusive thought
or finding an eye for detail
instead of keeping pace

we may hear
the flicker and chatter
of wild Honesty
see snow-covered fields
steaming in the heat
of the Indiana sun.

Power of words

A welling of tears,
of heartache
listening to 'Imagine'
wanting   the world to be
peaceful – no more

refugees...
their eyes fearful,
tired,
trudging to a camp
 so large

they will be insignificant.

And we still want to hear
a plea for peace, and tolerance
of each other,
a palpable stillness.

We live in our own bubble
of love; everything around us
breathing beauty,
though will the world ever be as one?

John Lennon sings, 'Imagine'

In the moment

It’s like the war
shops closed down
too many people walking about
jobless, she thought.

Disregarding the depressing
even the homeless lady
dressed in black sitting
on the pavement.

She flips open her coat collar
feeling the sun’s warmth and
only halfway through winter
it’s as if she had been

presented with a gift.
Small mercies accepted.
Nothing would bring
her down now.

Intimidated

She wouldn’t go
any further, couldn’t
break the rules;
‘stay alert’.

Sky blue, gentle breeze
a day to be brave
shout at the Corona;

to frighten the Devil
driving fear
into the infirm
undeserving
of his scourge.

Will our time come
again as before
enjoyed, free
as birds – no cares,

gentle in mind
with loving stirring hearts?

Changing course

Warnings set minds to worry.

A tornado touches down close by,
brings us to the edge; it could twist closer.

But safe under the house
as storms crash, light up the sky,
we wait out the night.

Somewhere else
the clouded fury devours towns,
spews debris A-frames split like tinder;
walls, ripped ply
roofs twist off.

There
threads of memory are scattered,
the spirit to weave another course
is lost in spin

though like a bud in darkness
pointing toward a glimmer of light
thoughts of the new push through.

Place your bets

Like shale carried to shore by a wave thrust,
words shout out, rushing to be recognised.
Watch the excitement dancing in her eyes;
she scrabbles letters, realising just
how instinct works, depend on it she must
where another might have overlooked the chance.
See the focussed face study in advance
balls in the frame, then out again, with trust
in himself, he knows he's headed for fame.
"Going for higher stakes? Double away,
time to give luck a free rein in the game!
Enjoy!" they shout, "place your bets. Ready, play!"
Wheel spinning faster, slower; it's the same.
What you do now is only for today

The Bones of the Island

A click and a flash capture
as we mount the aged steps
of the Giant's Causeway.

We lurch on
on a wind-swayed rope bridge
eighty feet above waves and
still we hunger
for the history of the Island.

Written in stone the story
of the Irish poor; their flight
from the potato famine.
There was no grieving caress
for their dead – only a shallow grave
and quicklime. Passing by
the dying on Fever Road
the able-bodied begin
the 'Beggar's walk'.

Mended in mind and body
the stronger forge new ways,
lightening hearts with all
they possess;
their dance, voices
in song and folk tales
in the charmed Irish brogue.

Seeing the light

Several times the need comes to her
to record the day. More now
than ever her notes serve to remind her.

Confidence returns
and her daily recollection
of him is minimal;
the last four years
a stepping forward to normality
and she remembers
her thoughts are only hers.

Trees comfort her in sunlight
as she notices different greens,
shapes, attitudes shadows,
each attribute matters
as never before;
she is alive to the world.

Minutes fill with actions,
consequences noted;
the richness of a baby's smile,
a colour marking the day,
birdsong ringing
out over the park
new joy to her listening.

Chasing away dark shadows

Rationed, or home-grown, food was as welcome
as the guest to a family occasion.
Eating egg sandwiches, children listened
in awe to corners of conversation,
a different impetus driving each episode.

Tinkling keys rose to the decisive
'If I Could Shimmy Like My Sister, Kate',
the base pulsating, giving the house renewed heart;
spirits lifted in spite of the blackout.

In what little space
squeezing together afforded, some danced
to 'Lille Marlene', shared glances
empathizing with the snatched romance
underneath lamplight outside.

Standing on her Uncle's feet
as he danced,
the child sensed rhythm,
hearing his whispered,
'One, two-three, one two-three.'

Autumn

leaves are down,
the ground is a kaleidoscope
of reds, yellows, orange.

So quiet,
as if someone is planning the season.

Now
she sits in the chatter
of the café
where news spreads

of the wild fires of Oregon;
no chance of holding out
for the hill-side dwellers,

she thinks. Then

on hearing of a friend scammed
then re-imbursed,

her face changes
to a forever smile.

Evening Passes

Skylarks, sprits of song
spiral up to the blue wash,
then dive to the ground, invisible.

At the tide's edge
small fingers tick off
the I-Spy pictures
of the claw-armed,
fast runners, and slippery scavengers,
scrabbling for cover
as we tower
above their rock pools.

Wavelets creep in, burble in shifting shale.
Mother of pearl glistens in upturned shells.
Cold foam trickles over plimsolled feet
the children inhale sharply,
the flow rises so fast, they retreat
to a safe distance
to begin over again.

Needs diverted

Your voice is gentle
stirs me to a day
already hours old. Breakfast
is lost in the moment
of a darting thrush
probing for his.
                                        And now

you are moving away.

I return home to see leggy plants
waving, calling for care;
weeds claim gaps between paving;
the lawn edging
dishevelled
as a punk haircut

and like a stream divided
our lives flow out
two different ways

Arriving Soon

Loud music alongside
a background pulse,
we finger tap, wait for the green.
Our minds not here at red lights,
but there with you
swamped by bedclothes,
stitches lacing your chest.

We wonder at your heart throbbing,
stopped and restarted in the surgeon's hand,
moments from yesterday,
still not with us today.

Hiccup

Maybe Mother slept a while
after working in the heat
the day her daughter rang.

Later the lack of contact
becomes the worry
she takes to bed.

E-mailing Daughter
to stave off the nagging
feeling; the Delta variant rages
like a forest fire there.

Here, now, looking out
she reads on a passing bus
'Keep calm, carry on.'

Forward

The first surprise; I like it,
caught in the moment
drinking coffee
under a blue sky
then wandering back,
I realise
nothing is lost to me.

Whatever happens now
like rolling through countryside,
dry lanes; heavy perfume
of woody blossoms
pregnant with newness;
dots of rainbow colour,
the wild flowers meandering
in shade and sun
make me more inquisitive.

Some things, existing in a bloody past,
used to terrify me,
but visiting small hamlets,
listening to dialects
feeling the strangeness
of a culture
belonging to centuries gone by,
has not.

I didn't die young, for instance
or lose myself mentally
though I could not talk
of my growing
Into a sojourn of silence
which took years to unfurl.

My only love
is the constancy
of a tomorrow
in future.